	DATE DUE		12/16
9/11/21			

Pebble® Plus

EXTREME EARTH

HIGHEST PLACES ON THE PLANET

by Karen Soll

CAPSTONE PRESS
a capstone imprint

Pebble Plus is published by Capstone Press,
1710 Roe Crest Drive, North Mankato, Minnesota 56003
www.mycapstone.com

Library of Congress Cataloging-in-Publication Data
Soll, Karen.
  Highest places on the planet / by Karen Soll.
    pages cm.—(Extreme earth)
  Includes index.
  ISBN 978-1-4914-8342-8 (library binding)
  ISBN 978-1-4914-8346-6 (pbk.)
  ISBN 978-1-4914-8350-3 (ebook PDF)
1. Physical geography—Juvenile literature. 2. Altitudes—Juvenile literature. 3. Extreme
environments—Juvenile literature. I. Title.
  GB58.S65 2016
  551.43'2--dc23   2015025593

Editorial Credits
Karen Soll, editor; Juliette Peters, designer;
Tracy Cummins, media specialist; Tori Abraham, production specialist

Photo Credits
Alamy: Urban Golob, 19; iStockphoto: Steve Krull, 9; Newscom: Harald von Radebrecht
imageBROKER, 15; Shutterstock: Cristian Zamfir, Cover Top, Daniel Prudek, Design Element,
1, 21, Dominik Michalek, 5, Graeme Shannon, 13, Han Vu, 17, Ivsanmas, Map,
Lenar Musin, Cover Bottom Right, LIUSHENGFILM, 11, Lukas Uher, 22, Michael Papasidero,
3, Vadim Petrakov, Cover Bottom Left, 7

Note to Parents and Teachers

The Extreme Earth set supports the Next Generation Science Standards related
to earth science. This book describes and illustrates climate and geography. The
images support early readers in understanding the text. The repetition of words
and phrases helps early readers learn new words. This book also introduces early
readers to subject-specific vocabulary words, which are defined in the Glossary
section. Early readers may need assistance to read some words and to use the
Table of Contents, Glossary, Read More, Internet Sites, Critical Thinking Using the
Common Core, and Index sections of the book.

Printed and bound in China.
007478LEOS16

TABLE OF CONTENTS

HIGH PLACES

What would it be like

at the top of a mountain?

Let's find out about some of

the world's highest places.

Look up and see water
that falls a long way.
The world's highest waterfall
is called Angel Falls.
It is in South America.

Angel Falls in Venezuela is 3,212 feet (979 meters) above sea level.

Leadville is in the Rocky Mountains.

It is also called Cloud City.

It is the highest city

in the United States.

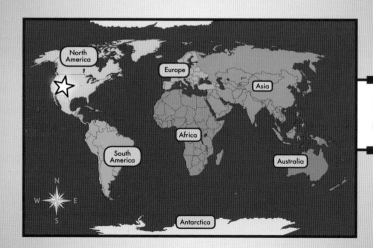

Leadville is 10,430 feet
(3,179 meters) above sea level.

HIGHER PLACES

People of the Tibet area
live on top of the world.
It is the highest place
people can live.

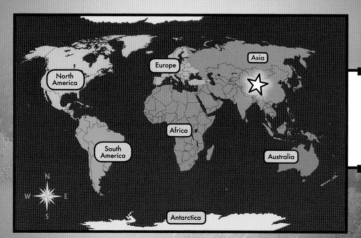

A village in Tibet is
16,730 feet (5,099 meters)
above sea level.

Mount Kilimanjaro is Africa's highest spot. Its peak always has snow and ice.

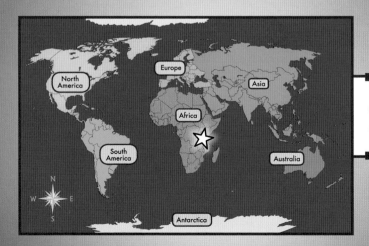

Mount Kilimanjaro is 19,340 feet (5,895 meters) above sea level.

HIGHEST PLACES

A volcano in South
America formed a lake
from rainwater. This is
the highest lake.

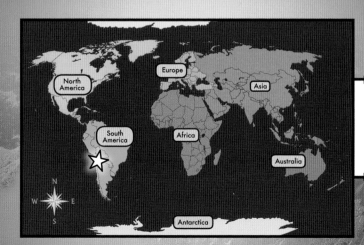

Licancábur volcano's lake is
19,409 feet (5,916 meters)
above sea level.

Where is the highest mountain

in North America? That is

Mount McKinley.

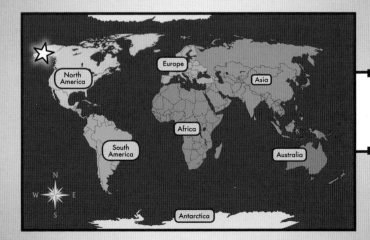

Mount McKinley is 20,320 feet
(6,194 meters) above sea level.

The second highest spot in the world is K2. K2 is in Asia. The mountain is rocky and snowy.

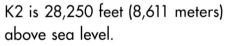

K2 is 28,250 feet (8,611 meters) above sea level.

The highest spot in the world
is Mount Everest. About
4,000 people have climbed it.
The world has many high places.
Which do you want to see?

Mount Everest is in the Himalayas.
It is 29,035 feet (8,850 meters)
above sea level.

GLOSSARY

area—a part

climb—to move upward

mountain—a very tall piece of land, higher than a hill

peak—the pointed top of a mountain

Rocky Mountains—a major mountain range in western North America

sea level—the average level of the surface of the ocean, used as a starting point from which to measure the height or depth of any place

volcano—an opening in the earth's surface that sometimes sends out hot lava, steam, and ash

waterfall—a place where river water falls from a high place to a lower place

READ MORE

Ganeri, Anita. *Harsh Habitats.* Extreme Nature. Chicago: Heinemann-Raintree, 2013.

Griffin, Mary. *Earth's Highest Places.* Earth's Most Extreme Places. New York: Gareth Stevens Publishing, 2015.

Hutmacher, Kimberly M. *Mountains.* Natural Wonders. Mankato, Minn.: Capstone Press, 2011.

INTERNET SITES

FactHound offers a safe, fun way to find Internet sites related to this book. All of the sites on FactHound have been researched by our staff.

Here's all you do:

Visit *www.facthound.com*

Type in this code: 9781491483428

Check out projects, games and lots more at
www.capstonekids.com

CRITICAL THINKING USING THE COMMON CORE

1. Why might Cloud City be a good nickname for Leadville? (Craft and Structure)

2. Use the pictures and the text to compare Mount Kilimanjaro to K2. (Key Ideas and Details)

3. Pick one of the high places in this book. Write about what you might see there. (Integration of Knowledge and Ideas)

INDEX

Grade: 1